Life is Perfect

Life is Perfect

Poems by
Amy Small-McKinney

BookArts Press
2013

Life is Perfect
Poems by Amy Small-McKinney

Copyright © 2013 by Amy Small-McKinney

All rights reserved.
No part of this book may be
reproduced or transmitted in any form
or by any means, electronic or mechanical,
including photocopying, recording,
or by any information storage and retrieval system,
without permission in writing from the publisher.

Published by

BookArts Press
www.book-arts-press.com

Design by Jon Pastor

Cover Artwork
Poet's Moon
mixed media collage
Copyright © 2012
by Helen Mirkil

ISBN 978-0-9795861-4-9

1.0.1

To Russ & Sarah

& for L, thank you

Table of Contents

    i Acknowledgements
  iii Author's Note

I. How It Is

  3 a talking to by my body
  5 Dillsburg, PA
  6 Clear Moon, Frost
  7 The Meaning of Life
  8 Life & Some Trees
10 When Your Eyes Darken
11 Something To Live On
12 A Walk
13 Brown Stars
14 So, This is How It Is
15 Snow Blind
16 Life is Perfect
18 Today I Wake
19 Letter From A Scarred & Aging Body
21 bats
22 After I Learned To Drive
23 Photo
24 Untitled
26 Found

II. To Speak To You

29 Barringer Street
30 OCD
31 Milk and Bones
32 The Tent
35 Eddie and His Beagle
37 Sisters

38 Parts of the Self
39 For Elsa
41 Trying To Speak To You

III. Okay

45 Two Figures Sitting & Walking
47 Music
49 Dreaming Ciechanowiec
52 Reading the News
53 Voices
58 Tuscaloosa
59 Celebrate
60 On My Knees
61 Not Yet
63 The Porch

~

65 Notes on the Poems
67 About the Author
69 Colophon

Acknowledgements

The author wishes to thank the editors of the following journals, in which versions of these poems have appeared, or will be appearing in forthcoming issues:

amphibi.us: "When Your Eyes Darken"

APIARY: "Parts of the Self"

Blue Fifth Review: "Letter From A Scarred & Aging Body"; "Music"; "Two Figures Sitting & Walking"

Bloomsbury Press: a portion of "Snow Blind" appeared in the novel, *The Wilderness*, author K. Novak

The Cortland Review: "Voices"

Elixir Press: "Snow Blind"

Finishing Line Press (chapbooks): "bats"; "Clear Moon, Frost"; "Dillsburg, PA"; "Eddie and His Beagle"; "Found"; "The Meaning of Life"

LIPS Poetry Magazine: "Sisters"

Mad Poets Review: "Clear Moon, Frost"

Massachusetts Poetry Festival, The Poetry Dress: "Snow Blind"

MiPOesias Magazine: "a talking to by my body"

OVS Magazine: "Barringer Street"; "Tuscaloosa"

Philadelphia Stories (Editor's Choice): "Not Yet"

Poetica: "Life is Perfect"

Rio Grande Review: "For Elsa"

r.kv.r.y. quarterly literary journal: "Dillsburg, PA"

SAND, Berlin's English Literary Journal: "Milk and Bones"

Schuylkill Valley Journal of the Arts: "Found"

Switchback, University of San Francisco: "Dreaming Ciechanowiec"

Umbrella: "A Walk"

***upstreet** magazine*: "Eddie and His Beagle"

A debt of immense gratitude to editor Meg Kennedy, artist Helen Mirkil, poet Liz Chang, the staff at BookArts Press, and to those who gave space and time to write this book: Trudy Hale at The Porches, Peter Murphy's gang at the Winter Poetry & Prose Getaway, and Joanne Leva and her Montgomery County Poet Laureate Program. Thanks also to two groups of poets without whom I may not have finished, Montco Poet's Wordshop and the Saturday regulars at Leonard Gontarek's house. I am grateful to Catherine Bancroft and David Kertis for their careful proofreading.

Author's Note

I remember the precise moment. I was in a wood paneled finished basement, a place that used to be called "the rec room," when I inadvertently picked up a poem, "Do Not Go Gentle Into That Good Night." I was, maybe, eight. Upstairs, I could hear the rumblings of family life, petty arguments, a kitchen fork pulled from a drawer, my brother's trucks scraping against a wood floor, the dog whimpering to go outside. I heard all of that, some, or maybe none; poetry allows memory to discover itself. What emerges, for me, is always true.

I sense that poetry allows me to remember parts of the whole and those parts are as important and urgent as the sum. It allows me to write from both the ordinary, that which I see and hear and touch, and the undisclosed, that which is between the handshake, the chair being pulled out, and greetings exchanged.

Writing allows me to become others. What may appear, at first blush, to be fully autobiographical, often has been jump-started by another's story, something I borrowed or stole, and my life and theirs become interwoven, almost indistinguishable, though I hesitate to presume or compare our lives. Poems allow me to reach beyond myself and inhabit the stories of others. Paradoxically, I am freed to return to my own story, my own memories, and finally, feel connected.

So, what have I told you? Poems help me to feel connected to others, less alone. They help me to assemble all the parts of myself.

When my own poems emerge, they are generally not narrative, but rather Chagall-like, where pieces of this or that enter the poem and find a place, unexpectedly, beside seemingly unrelated pieces. These are never dreams. I sometimes imagine a tiny conductor with her wand somewhere smack in the center of the brain's cortex. How else to describe the comings and goings of all of these images and voices?

Muriel Rukeyser said, "Poetry does invite, it does require. What does it invite? A poem invites you to feel. More than that: it invites you to respond. And better than that: a poem invites a total response." I thank poetry, and readers, for inviting me in.

What supports me? I have forgotten
from where I come and where I'm headed,
in several bodies I live on,
a hard thorn and the deer that fled.

>   Ingeborg Bachmann,
>   Translated by Peter Filkins,
>   from *How Shall I Name Myself?*

1.

How It Is

a talking to by my body

or rather now you are a farmhouse—
sloping walls durable tin roof
a few nails popped
like heads of cabbage

talking to you comforts me
miles between us level into fields
i tell you a sparrow consumes a cow
you say a cow walks into a bar

as we stroll toward a bleeding forest
though I know you are willing to be glass
or a glass of red wine
someone you love can drink

and not stop
until sated
or rather you are willing to be
untilled fields where sparrows

gather to discuss weather
your heart unstable
knows where it belongs
where we belong

you are still my sweetheart
since before your hair was bobbed
you might have been born in Poland
wished you had posed for Modigliani

then you were lanky as a conscience
until the baby awoke you at 3 am

banging to be heard
unlike the others

she traveled with you
her tattered case stamped at the train
now you wait for a sign
from an indifferent ovary

you will wait some more
for an expanse of acreage
let me be blunt for living and dying
storm warning or eye of a storm

i am sorry
fear is a cup of tea
you do have to drink

"okay body i am listening"

Dillsburg, PA
for Pui

The frogs have begun whistling.
Black Walnut trees, their green globes
the size of tennis balls, have not begun to shed,
or to make their mess, though they secret
walnuts inside. There is a retention pond,
not useful any longer, but once good for fire,
if one happened nearby, or for thirsty cattle.
Now it is moss, chomped through branches
carpet its surface, probably poisoned by juglone.
I imagine, like to imagine, below
there is ancient water, water that is glass clear,
where my dead daughter can drink and murmur
along with the frogs. I imagine, beneath the jade
smut and decay, the story of every person
who has ever visited this house, who has ever
tucked the sheer curtain behind the brass leaf,
opened a window, at least once, for air or to look away
from a stupid mistake made over and over, the story
of every person who has needed to hear the high pitched
whistles and squeaks, is gathered, and finally understood,
while the frogs offer the only advice possible—
Listen.

Clear Moon, Frost

How I have used
the vowel's scalpel

How I heard scraping on the sill
and swore it was fear

How you tried to tell me
of forgiveness

How I have come to love the leaf
at my window the mouth that disappears

The Meaning of Life

I am happy when I find the juicy orange.
I am happy when the sofa is on sale,
happiest when I have not lost my job.
I have turned off the news, thrown
away the papers—I know this world.
I wake, spy my slippers, my robe,
shake my child to school, to soccer, to bed.
I dream of strangers, fiery objects flaming my home
and huge questionable birds
flapping hungrily over my roof.

Life & Some Trees

My husband plants Lemon Boy Hybrids, tomatoes, seventy-two days to produce.
In the meantime, tattooed newcomers pull trucks onto a neighboring lawn.
I call my brother and say, *I cannot live without you, at times.*

In the meantime, which one of us will lift a bag of soil?
Bend with a trowel during our fifteen minutes of green?
Note the Lilies of the Valley that return in spite of our neglect?

My brother lives outside of Boston in a glass house bounded by unruly foliage.
We argued while mother was dying. Announced, in case she heard,
"Don't worry, we love each other."

Later, I will listen for the sounds of my husband upstairs,
a kind of slide to synthetic moccasins,
no matter how many years I request shoes off in the house.

Do you know that Japanese green leaves are the maple's most delicate?
Never about content, is it, these startling skirmishes.

～

When I was sixteen, I had a crush on Rossano Brazzi
who charmed a young woman by a fountain.

What happens when the one I love is an outline
or almost a shadow? Rather, I anticipate
an awkward gray being glimpsed at a particular angle,
full sun behind.

～

There was a long line of trees, reminding us of a boulevard
where we could imagine.
On the third tree,

very pale blossoms had refused to bloom
its first two years. It waited,
as we waited, to find each other.

∼

My city— somewhere else, an immense forest,
ice on trees, untied hair.
I am alone now and when someone knocks, undressed.
My body feels as though I am eighty, no older, I am not.
If I were tattooed with faces I love, I might forget the inconsequential.
My dead mother wants me to wave the stranger in.
In the meantime, I cannot reach the door.
If I open, someone will remember to take everything:
the green velvet chair, orange throw, remaining tetras.
Or what I really mean: *swallow* my life.

∼

My whole life, I have tried to explain space between motifs.
Mimosa leaves that close to the touch, indelible mouths, I am tired.

How to build a bridge across a gorge?
I am mother of a twenty year old, wife to a man almost seventy-five.

When he returns, my dear will fall asleep with his shoes on.

When Your Eyes Darken

You wait, wrapped inside your blanket,
your eyes, black ponds.
I strike against ice, long to swim
the waters of each.
I am afraid of everything, and this nothing.
Are you behind those eyes?
A curator once showed me a cranium,
its plate-like bones, a look
into what had once been, imagined.
Palm opened, I touch your face.
I link us with a string, conjured at night,
in the dark. Do you know?
Ice fishing into you, I love
the fact of Spring.

Something To Live On

Luke wants to sell the rental filled with boys.
The new owner will restore. We won't be fined.
Money reinvested—something to live on.
My cousin is right. I am dense about money.
Picture myself selling roses on Market.
No one will know me. (By then my Beth will be content.)
Teeth will surely go first. The lower right where grinding
polishes them to white corn. Then my womb wall
that inexplicably thickens. Next week I will be the sea.
My doctor with her contraption a submarine inside of me.
The part of my body I still love. Luke floats far away.
Pain is not a distant swallow.
I listen to the stories of my students.
Fathers sleep with them mothers dead drunk the kids
slice into their wrists and thighs.
One hurt replaces another.
Today Beth comes home for a visit.
Luke will sleep until noon.
Outside a reliable sky.

A Walk

Because I have no answers,
I walk. Away from the house
with yellow shutters and toward
magnolias that drop like egg shells.
Toward music of consent, language
of ascent. I think of her as petal
resigned against blacktop. Head bowed
in bony prayer. Without her,
I am an orphan laborer; I envy
the leaves that fall and never doubt
their own falling. Remarkably, the layers
of this self hold; the wind, almost too robust
for the boxwood trees, holds. This morning,
two massive limbs stretch towards us—
me and the she I carry inside of me—someone
secured them, pinioned them like wings.
Nearby, a green necked mallard marauds
a suburban lawn. How did he get here?
Alone and close to cars? I walk. Until
feather light. Until there are no losses.

Brown Stars

After the court's decision, after I signed the usual papers.
I recall tossing the Bloodroot I tried to grow. Though known
to dry up with one watering missed. I once heard a story
about a town where the women would throw themselves
against grain and something invisible would kiss
them but nothing not even the kiss was remembered.
Nine months later. A baby born meant a year without famine.
Sweety found the baby. Eyes brown stars in the center
of coats and boots. Theresa counseling a mirage.
Twenty years later, I remember Sweety, Theresa, the baby.
The smooth white blanket, its rocking horses galloping away.

So, This is How It Is

I was born in a cave. I want to return.
Crystal sheets of predictable ice,
the occasional multi-celled tardigrade, Arctic algae.
Who can trust humans?
Yes, I manage, but inside the raw milk
of recall, glass, a slow moving car,
a whistle somewhere heading toward a porch,
I remain cold, separate.
Who can trust them?
They dream of love the way they dream of life on distant, freezing planets.
How do I know one won't scale a building, leap away in longing?
Or waste her life frozen inside her satin bed?
Who knows if one won't hold up a bank, or me, at gunpoint
for the jewels I have never owned?
Or breathe into me as though I am a paper bag?
Or marry me?
All of this is conjecture and possible.

Snow Blind
for K

Nothing changes, exactly.
No subliming of elements.
Nothing as malleable as silver, fluid as mercury;
memory's body is not that solid.
I know. You have heard this before—
but for this woman, this rock and field,
this blur of body's suggestion, matter shifting
as she would shift; here, everything begins.
Snow, let me lie in your drifts. No eyes nor rings,
dark and marking time. I will be birch white; I will be snow blind.

Inside this snow, a scurf of birch
breathes memory and breathes again.
Nothing returns; nothing is the sky
and the earth that drinks the snow, and the snow
that falls unreasonably and certain.
Leaf of absolution, sky of gladness,
there is no need for chemistry.
I am your despair. Now return to what is real.
Everyone you have ever loved, or almost loved, is here.

Life is Perfect

I tell my daughter that life is perfect
because it is imperfect.
I heard my daughter tell a friend
who did not understand
that because she is imperfect
she is perfect.
I tell my daughter that when something
a molecule or an atom is stable
it deserves to be named.
I named my daughter Sarah
because I was old and was told
I could not carry her and I did
because she was perfect
and deserved to be named.
On Sunday morning over coffee I show my daughter
a facsimile of Picabia's painting Kiss.
I show her the white snowy smudges that become his hair
the long black nose that becomes her mouth
the embroidered sleeve that becomes her hair
and tell her, "This is not the real thing
but it is all that we've got."
I tell her that we have to love what we are given—
the molecules or atoms that stabilize
into ourselves our family our school our friends
the stop sign where we stand together
hand in hand each morning the traffic
that infuriates us with its thoughtlessness
the peeling ceiling that needed paint two years ago
the dying dog who refuses to die
the rosy mole she calls her strawberry
that sprouts above her right eye

because she caught like a dusking hummer
tossed her way my genes and my fears
that catch her at night and demand duplication
before they dissolve back into their destined cradle.
All of this all of this we had better just love.
Even the thorny locust trees that we can barely
tug apart from the elegant hostas
because those trees push up and out
against our limey soil and drought hardened earth
in spite of our yearnings
in spite of who we become.

Today I Wake

Ordinary, except the azaleas are in bloom.
They are purple. The dead ones have returned
with pruning and not much else.
I don't care, except when I look out from my window,
brew dark roast, try to haul myself to work,
they are there, a surprise party, no congratulations.
They remind me of gratitude.
How does someone do it?
Live in New York and recall details of surprise,
the black plow's outline below a sunset?
I have trouble remembering anyone,
let alone the boy with black hair in a green tent
near New Hope, behind our tacky apartment.
It was always summer.
The boy in the tent, we were cicadas.

Letter From A Scarred & Aging Body

Dear X,

This is my ankle. Its slit of infinite *e*.
This is my belly. Its brittle scab
Of question mark. I told you
About the car that buckramed
Into mine. I do love these breasts
Suckled nearly two years.

Still I disappear

Need I disappear?

∼

I love the brown brick buildings. Limestone.
Do you?

My daughter and I. Light swipes
A silver door. Someone is singing:
Oh What A Beautiful Morning.
We walk quickly because he is tone deaf
And annoyed. We walk quickly

Though notice the boy with black hair
Notice her and I remember

A boy with black skin

Lifting my skirt.

I remember everything now.

Everything

～

Inside this body—
Memory—
The hokey song
Inside the scar.

It promises
I will remain
Light against your door.

Its promises
Are not to be believed

As always, A

bats

this is not about trees or clouds or birds
i am not the white salver

i toss across my white kitchen sky splintered
i once loved it i am baffled by extinction oh I need

the wild to gather in ten thousand years from out of ice
to return to a bracken cave to need you as

my fifth wing-finger this is not about becoming the sky
maybe it is how to become a sliver how to roost

near the sweet cluster dangle from your mindful ceiling
imagine learning my voice my scent in less than one hour

this is not about becoming another night no sleep
my body who am I

After I Learned To Drive

The car smelled of lemon.

I wanted to be lost.

I had already lost my name.

I wanted to drive myself.

Leave me on the side of a road.

I drove toward the family tree.

How could I not?

My body was grandfather's evening joke.

Well, yes, I had hope.

It became liquor, neat.

Uncle is what I called you.

I was your sea cave.

You were thirsty.

I was your Riviera,

headlamps beneath clamshell doors.

Now I name everything: hubcap, finger, breast, despair, radio.

I drive away from you.

I don't know where I am going.

I hold the moon,

it at least is mine,

in my hand.

Photo

Black & White

Behind her are pine trees, evergreens, pine trees.
I want to say *shines*.
A barber shaped her hair beneath a bowl.
She squeezes arms against her sides. Her white shirt:
Blue Mountain Camps. The waist of her shorts too high.

She is paradox.
Her cheeks though thin puff out.
Chiclets from Pop-Pop on visiting day.
He is probably whistling Glow Worm as he shoots.
She is thin as bark whittled into a boat.

Rowing Across

Please let me choose another photo:
Daughter. Brother. Anyone can use a poem.
I can't tell her I am sorry.
Little kid this is what will happen. Strangers.
Lovers. For awhile, you will not know who you are.

There was a lake. She rowed across
until a counselor called come back.
I should row today toward adventure.
I should row today toward her.
My oars skim the surface.

Untitled

I will talk to you about a man that fell.
A husband sprawled beside a mower.
How his body almost becomes tall grass.
How I have begun to accept miracles.
To pray for the slim boy I knew who knew love.
His body a blossom that drifted into my hands.

Seconds are sprinters helpless in my hand.
Where is my hand no the hand I held when I finally fell?
It was inside The Kosciuszko House when I sensed love.
Now my house is dust towels a rusty mower.
Then I believed in unreasonable miracles.
While my husband waits in the grass.

Look I want green white dogwood unruly grass.
Even doubt that lines my hand.
Believe me when I say being alive is a miracle.
In that second was paradise there when he fell?
Beside him that stupid machine the mower.
Damn it we rode away from one another our love.

There is a kind of rhythm in my house of love.
At times I hear it in plates or grass.
When I write the checks drive the mower.
At night dream of someone's mouth and hand
and in that dream imagine my husband fell
into my body my language of miracle.

Into memory and recognition of daily miracles.
As though arthritis and heart surgery sing of love.
Together into the stretch of hope we fell.
Into the unruly indestructible grass.

Inside my crotch inside years ago his hand.
Everything the rake and mower.

Then sweet John our neighbor hauls the mower.
Returns to lift my husband one small miracle.
I watch from the window as he draws him into his hand.
I believe I am watching love.
Because of the tender mouth the quiet grass.
Everyone understands the meaning of fell.

The mower dragged they walk from where he fell.
Purple wildflowers tuft of grass slim miracles.
I don't go to him don't offer my hand believe me this is love.

Found

All of these years I have lived without you and now
you slip like light beneath my door.

Light glides toward me. Everything else is gray.
Even the tree branch bending close to

my house is gray. All color gone.
I lift up the light. It gathers in my hands.

11.

To Speak To You

Barringer Street

I want to speak to the new neighbor, tell her I don't want to disappear.
Tell her the maple is almost perfect. Like Hal's legs swollen and zipped
with staples. What is perfect about skin bound in metal? Hal is alive.
I promise. I will haul away the limbs. Become a decibel breaking open.
To be precise, I will make decisions. The neighbor is working
beside what is becoming a highway.

Bent by the lamppost, lit from within, she is scooping leaves.
As though she cannot hear cars passing. There are earthworms I am sure
and sweet creatures I can't name. She doesn't give a damn.
They are alive. I know. I will sneak in at night throw the ashes
on top of the carved hands praying. Or, are they a steeple?
I will bring a flashlight. A rabbi. Imagine life without.

Remember early summer's tree? Massive roots wrapped around a boulder?
The trail is marked. I will not lose myself. I will make it beyond
to the waterfall, the fullness. Everything grows toward light.
The woman who is a window looks up. She doesn't smile.
(How much can we expect?) Hal becomes noun and verb for wick.
Wick—as in Dickon finds a garden. As in fiber becoming flame.

I don't want to disappear. I know. I will tell them—
You are what I have found. You, who are now.

OCD

It begins with ease, count to ten,
ten not enough, try fifteen,
return to one, grip the oven knob.
Whisper: off and off and off.
Your hand is not a hand.

The girl who washes your hair has hair that swirls
inside a breeze. No breeze in this salon.
The woman with foils inherited a home.
In Le Marche she would rent,
imagine barricades of vineyards.

Could you live with the Cirl Buntings' endless singing?
Is there an oven in Spinetoli?
Imagine the sun,
it slows the basil ganglia.
Tonight you simply inch in and out of bed.

Each time you embark your blanket shifts.
Your body is a breeze. Sleep no comfort.
Your house might burn.
The one you love could die at seven.
Line up in sweet formation.
All possibilities!
Geese fly south.

Milk and Bones

Do you know that in Sudan, 72 pounds means, *still alive?*
My mother waits for me. She is starving.
She refuses to walk outside. It is a country of chance and confusion.
Rests her head on the silk pillow my aunt brought from her travels.
Look, I know nothing about Sudan. I read its children, the diamonds
they pan for scraps of bread. My mother remains another mystery.
Here in America my mother survives where only buses have disappeared.
She welcomes dying as she might brie and wine.

The Tent

In a green plastic tent with yellow stripes on its back, the gray haired woman
counts pennies, each coin collected years ago, lost and gained,
because inside this tent, the child's tent, everything returns, sooner or later.

The voice of Adonai convulses the wilderness.

I remember when the child only slept in a tent set up in her room
with three stuffed animals, including a yellow bear with a red vest, a white
bear holding a small red heart in its hand, and of course, you already guessed,
a zebra with one eye missing. I would arrange myself beside the tent and sing,

Your Feets Too Big, at least three times, before the air around me
calmed and I could also sleep.

At the sleepover, by the pool, my air mattress flattened each time
I tried to rest, but with three girls giggling intonations of boys' names,
my body gave way to when I almost lost you.

This is not about tents, is it?

Canada was wild even in the spring, and our tent held us as it might a child and you decided,
then and there, you loved me, but wanted to head home west, leaving me
to return to the east, a first floor studio, windows barred.

I know there is a book about a red tent, but I have never read beyond the first chapter.
Maybe I already know her and her water always following from the well.

When Els died, I wanted to be her, I mean the woman in the tent.
I wanted to be a tent, a portable feast, and follow into the world
of welcoming tambourines and men with brilliant hands.
I am not dead yet. Isn't everything about this?

Who is this, rising up from the desert?
Who is she, rising up?

I loved the tent we kept in the living room. She would color all of the blank spaces
shaped like dogs and cats and bears. I crawled down with her and loved the blues best.
Even today, though green is now my favorite, I know it is the family of teals and turquoise.

Because the bluish sky stretches into my mouth, words are still rough.

In a farmer's truck, when we stopped in Iowa,
the driver said the Jews were taking over his land,
and you held my hand, but I wanted to kill him.
It was the first time, well, I knew I would go home.

That night, in the tent, you whispered not to be afraid and the stars were cups of water.
I loved and refused you.

A thought has blown the market place away…Eternity utters a day.

Why not be friends? A joke of course, since it was all about loathing,
until I forgave myself, and I will not tell you, here and now, why.
Don't ask. In the gray tent, where my dog named Sabra barked all night,
you surprised me. You did not throw her over the cliff.

My father wears a plastic fireman's hat and his pale blue robe when he climbs inside
on his veined legs and swollen feet to play with her. He squeezes
beside my mother as she points out each coin, its year, and reason for being.

Miriam, let me enter your tent now.
Let my body never be cups of blood.
I will live in your tent. I am a rock. I am a hard place. I will eat only grapes.

I have heard that grapes turn to vinegar.

The green tent with yellow stripes, beneath stacks of amnesia,
has a yellow flapped entrance, with the words, "Keep Out" painted on a tree house,
and a toothy frog grinning with secrets.

If you construct a tent with grapes, my table will fall in love with you.
Though oak, children believed it was paper and I have sliced cantaloupes
and onions for someone I loved more than I imagined.
I will build in the morning.
It will be small enough to move anywhere. It will not be a hospital.

I always wanted to have small breasts like grapes, red and seedless. What I have are cantaloupes with splendid soggy seeds. You have to love me to understand. Or come to my tent.

Eddie and His Beagle
for Tim Suermondt

My friend the poet has his father,
Eddie from Vegas, living with him now
along with his misbehaving beagle
who pulls poor fumbling Eddie down the concrete
sidewalks of Queens where no royalty resides
and my friend the poet watches as Eddie dissolves
into a world we all know is coming
and still never expect.

I watched my own father sneak away
still furious at the end, his body frozen,
except his hands
that he moved like dancers,
or engineers, what he lived for—
years of useless repairing.

Is that what you think: This is a boring story?
Think all you want, but plan to be pulled
by your old and winded beagle.
If he is given away or put down
and you are housed in a warehouse
for shrinking frontal lobes,
he will search for you;
you'll call your nurse
by his name, you'll hear his bark,
sparks will fly between you
and your son or your daughter,
then fade inaudibly away.

In the meantime, Eddie
will tell his son, my friend the poet,

what my father, still dead, tells me,
what I need to tell my daughter,
all she will need to know:
walk the dog,
turn off the stove,
I'll see you in the morning.

Sisters
for B

Summer. Not really, early spring.
We are building a fence to erase our neighbors,
four pit bulls, a snake, a raccoon, a tent
and laundry waving on the front lawn, here in the suburbs
where we tried to give our child a life as simple as pudding.
Can I forgive them?
Our house is worth far less now, our future in doubt.
I remember the winter when my sister slammed my face
into a snowdrift, its stunning white ice.
Well, I forgive her, almost, my sister,
though we don't speak and have not for years. We grow older.
Not because of snow. Certainly not weather or dogs.
What does it remind me of?
Love rationed, dear as air.

Parts of the Self

I was raised in a family of nothing creators,
inside, outside, belonging, disowned.
In Reva's jeweled box, there were photos
with black crayon smeared across banned faces.
I will never know resemblances, if they wrote poems
in Odessa or preferred green apples.
Samantha drew the same black across our parents,
our brother, his wife, daughter, my daughter, me.
With a swipe, our mouths, suspicious blackbirds.
Someone is always furious, rummages for love
from rationed cans on nearly empty shelves.
Greta cut out my mother, her daughter, from the will,
my mother sliced my sister Sam.
There is always war, what is left is a stencil.
At the end, my mother sang, *shine little glow worm*.
I am aging, unravel as stretched paper,
I cannot trust anyone.

For Elsa

1. Learning a House

Moved into six months before.
The house in the woods.
The swing set. The couch.
The Barn Owl. At night,
we listened. I learned plantains.
I learned sugar and salt. To become
a feather. To drift away.

2. Learning a New Language

I promised my brother
I would return: I would draw
circles with his daughter.
Water drawn from a child's well.
At night, I would rock her,
learn: *Dios te salve, María*.
Name the Owl, then sing to him.
What I learned: Love her.

3. How Mamacita Looked

She was desert.
Her breasts, disappearing.
Her face: nose and teeth and sockets.
Her mouth, disappearing.
One grunt for ice, another for daughter.

4\. The Child and I Drive Away

Years of revolt, then my brother
asked for a Rabbi.
The sisters: *Por favor Dios.*
That night, I wrapped her foo foo
and blanket into the ballet bag,
tried not to wake her. I did.
We drove to Uncle Steve's.
Mamacita didn't die until morning.

5\. Traditions of Stones

I want to talk about stones. Stones
do decay, but with elegance, belief.
Then I would have to talk about the pit,
how each stone tossed in was a heart.
One became snow.
The stone made me cry, I remembered
New Year's. She asked me to sing.
It was too late—for stone or song.
The world was parched.
Who will grill the dry, green plantains?
Each morning, in Boyacá, my mother
carted bowls to the well.
The well followed Miriam home, damn it.

Trying To Speak To You

Finally, I died, which took longer than I expected. I waited for you.
Am I talking to you? Does it matter?
Even when alive you refused to return to the kitchen table or into my dreams.
For years, you were seabirds coming and going. Now I know that all that we
        carry with us in
life follows us, until we are safe. Don't believe: Less is more or that you are not
        everything.
Everything returned. The yellow curtain, its kindest purple leaves.
Aunt Henrietta's *Art Nouveau— Jugendstil* (Was I ever *young art?*)—you
        probably loved until the whole world was lithographs, until you were
        engraved
into the one called, *Death Seizes a Woman*.

111.

Okay

Two Figures Sitting & Walking

It is in that thought that we collect ourselves...
      - Wallace Stevens, "Final Soliloquy of the Interior Paramour"

Everyone spoke Spanish at the Grove Street
Grocery Store established 1953.
Massive burritos, gargantuan, stuffed
with spicy rice with seasonings
we hadn't tasted before.

~

Somewhere everything makes sense
and I love without my usual greediness
or so I imagine.

Because: *It is in that thought that we collect ourselves.*

Because: *It is not possible to float and watch the stars while drowning.*

~

Food as despair/delight:
Even now my dead father demands I devour everything.
Even now my late sister-in-law prepares plantains
buried in salt and oil.

At Grove Street, we ate together.

~

Okay. Okay.

I tell you again because it is remembered
as true &
we move toward a river.

You ask: *Is that a body floating face up?*

Had I the nerve I would have said:
Does she notice the stars?

I do not understand why
your hand reminds me of hunger.

Music

I wrote a song in my sleep
I can't remember.

Something about my body.
What music do you hear when afraid?

It was soft, but not too soft,
at times almost Vivaldi,

though no excessive optimism.
Partly Cohen, frogging his Hallelujah,

accepting the slightest of nothing.
Because I have written in my sleep,

because I am not a musician,
they were simple chords,

space between family
or space between notes—

Manacha lobbed into a Polish pit,
Ben, shushed inside a stinking ship—

the world's dissonance
before Monk & *I don't know.*

Now here I am—another aging woman.
What or who are these tunes that won't leave me?

Hands that clap with the Barry Sisters,
as though those sirens would return everything.

If I could begin with hands.
In my dream, my hands floated away,

bright blue, almost aqua, and a black sketch of an animal
over my shoulder, everything floating,

as though we would never land safely.
Do you remember following music of a bouncing ball?

I cannot find my body.
It has become a wavelength of sound or the ting

of a triangle in the back row.
It has become blood captured behind a macula.

Everything once linear now swells.
I listen for my body as a burglar breaking in.

Tonight I will listen to songs about belonging.
There will be a guitar and one drum.

Some I will remember from long ago,
distracted in a hard chair.

Some I will hum or pretend to know,
because they are sweet songs about light and hearts.

I am trying to tell you something and I am afraid.
I never expected you to listen this hard.

I will wake you if I dream the song again.

Dreaming Ciechanowiec
The Synagogue of Ciechanowiec... It is an empty building...

The mole on the skin—
I remember watching the shoulder
above me slant toward the sun.
It is best to remember only parts of the sum—
sweat spilling off of a body,
a blacksmith awl searing into skin.

In my skin, you rise
and in my dreams
you demand:

Today is no different.
Today is not another day.

Outside,
the branch that fell
from the maple
is dragged
with indifference.
I do not turn once
to watch them haul
the stricken limb away.

Inside,
I turn twice.
He carries me over
his shoulder.
The others—his mother,
her mother, the mother before—
follow us into the driveway,

into the green Chevrolet,
into our day as we planned it.

Night riddle:
Where are the lovers, sisters, brothers, neighbors?

Listening for Schönberg,
his Survivors from Warsaw,
before he composed it.

Choose. Choose.
Remember us.

It is too late to choose.
My life is being led
as I dream you,
it will end
soon enough.
My father is dead.
He died a year ago
from modern disease.
The slap, the stare,
the fist raised above
with a hunter's grief
are gone.

Black bib of memory, comfort of dreams,
smooth scent, sound—the lace collar against a chin—
how she dressed when she wasn't dressing
horses with poultice for thrush, gashes.

This is her horse,
its shoe perfect against its pad,
black eyes beneath brown fringe:

You are not who you are supposed to be.

"You are right."

Ciechanowiec: The Bialystok District of Poland

Reading the News

Because sitting here in this chair by this window
light shoving its way past the breeze shifting maple—

No one can eat imagination.
(& light is not water)

Or notice the way
a mouth

implores
a moon.

Then closes
against the *Xagaa*.

How low trees refuse
to defend against a commotion of rifles.

The world becomes another *Naja haje*.
And language is not enough.

Because only in imagination
they will not die.

Voices

Provincetown, USA

What I love most is morning.
My line cast for stripers,
their obedient mouths.
The girl was pretty, tall, lean enough.
In the graveyard, the headstones
shut their eyes, she could not hear
their sympathy. I heard her *No*,
but who can stop
in the throes of opening?
I do not wake every morning
and thank God I am a man.
That was another life.

Rwanda, Africa

Lake Kivu plaits through the Rift valley.
I was the Hutus' favorite daughter,
Pauline Nyiramasuhuko. My mouth
a volcano, a danger to anything
that breathed. My nation insisted
I become their nation, scissors opened
and closed. I sent my son, Shalom,
to young Rose with the Tutsi name—
A Plea to God—to where she hid, the fields
where she fought back.
I called to the Tutsis, exhausted as rain:
Here is your food. Here is your shelter.
All of their death took only an hour;
a red chested cuckoo asked why.
I told him: My eyes are split open.
I am not sorry.

Merewala, Pakistan

Sometimes, I still hear her in the shallow waters
of the Indus. She was never my true child,
my snow white crane, entreating me, *Feed me, Faz Mai.*
The sustenance that might have called her home
was only rain, this child who floated out of me
into a blister of nothing.
And my cousin Naseem, like me, forced to spread
herself into our country of dread, into the fields
where white bulbs of cotton were dying.

Massachusetts, USA

I blamed myself, my body, how dutifully
I inhaled an era. I did not blame him,
refused to remember the Portuguese stones of loss,
the nearby sea smacking its futile fish,
or later, how it slipped into the waters
of the Holiday Inn—my thumb nail, my lily.
Naseem Mai, then, I wanted to be you, wanted pesticide
to flow through my body like fresh milk.
Now I am milk. Now, another son has eyes so blue.

Bombay, India

This will never end, my wandering
out of my Bombay backyard where peafowl
sashay to the males' courtly *help help*
of recognition. I miss them more
than mother or father, their sendoff basket
of fruit. When the males release their plumage,
they call *ahhh ahhh*. The peahen mutters
Hell-o Hell-o.
I cannot tell you what you want to hear,
cannot remember the travelers' eyes, faces, words,
any kindnesses as I drifted out of my skin,
as my mouth became the rapist's chick, wingless, blind.
This will never end.

Tuscaloosa

Here is the premise. Let me assure you.
I have thought this through. First,
a finger on the globe. Find storm and neighborhood.
Perhaps, a thigh beneath a piano. A mouth

almost inside a magnolia. A white scarf. Its lullaby.
Then, how to say—exhausted?
Hope as I do for a slice of radiance, to remember love.
The premise? How sadness travels.

How it refuses to leave home.

Celebrate

On the front page, a soft pink shirt and her face shines.
I know. Shines is not the word. Hands reach for her
as though she is a goddess and she tells them:
*We haven't seen each other for so long. I have
so much to tell you.* Amazed is the word.

Because she made something of a life
in spite of house arrest. Because what we make
of ourselves is never what we imagined.
won't you celebrate with me what i have shaped into a kind of life
the poet asks and we answer: Always.

What is here, in this house, amazes me. I am telling the truth.
Never what I expected, never, but it folded into me—
shapes and always a kind of likeness to real life—
sometimes, I even see you, hands that have not touched me
for so long, and I have no choice, do I, except to celebrate.

On My Knees
for my brother

Someone should rename this act.
I mean the one where I am on my knees
reaching far beneath a dresser
and find my child's second grade drawing of a sun
with a face and flower hair and filth I have been living
with for years.

I cannot be alone in this. The need to begin again.
Aging brings with it not just cracks in my feet and impossible night driving.
It brings cardboard wardrobes I fill with only what is required.
I toss a velvet dress I called elegant. I remember how he looked at me.
Burgundy became my body. I was his wine. Now it refuses
to fit over these hips that carried my child. I called her *my package*.
And the wedding shoes I did not dye.

Loved their pale silky white. How they reflected the white beading
of my bodice. How my father said I was so beautiful he could not breathe.
And this clutch of hair. Now only a strand or two in an envelope I label Baby.
What do I do with these photos? I wonder at orderly people who have marked
each year. Mine are thrown together. Every year becomes the next.
I have lived my life like this. Not in stages but as a river.

I was drowning and sometimes I was sure someone
a guardian spirit perhaps held me. And I in turn held those
I loved. Not elegantly. Kneeling and reaching. Throwing out
what I called my mistakes and keeping close
what I could live with. What do I call this now?
Love, memory? No, just kneeling into my life.

Not Yet

if there is one thing I know
it's this storm how rain sloshed over
my bedroom floor boards ants swam to the island
of my black sandal onto a gray towel I brought from the Home

I had to haul out everything in two days
that was the rule they said & today I read how an amoeba
from a warm river attached to his tiny brain he died too my god
this morning everyone is asleep & I wonder how much of my life

is held inside these legs always skinny the boy whose arm
was around my shoulder told me more than twice & yes for a while I broke
& still these legs found their way to the well-lit bridge the Danube
the white blouse with blue swans across a boulevard

to the black Paris hat so ordinary no matter how much I tugged
the entire world was velvet except for the wooden house in Poland
where two women feared I had come back in brown dresses their hair wrapped
in buns they wanted me to leave wanted me out of their town I wasn't taking

anything I told them & Agneska told them & thank goodness
I knew to knock on the manager's door at the London guest house
though after midnight she offered tea of course in her blue robe
& I had been crying

she said I could not tell not done she would be fired it was strong
dark & perfect & these legs spindles for straw into gold
found their way home to my window where beyond yellow
curtains with burgundy leaves the storm split

my maple in two my country split

& upstairs neon pink stripes & dream above your bed
your mouth your breathing the wind
as though the world is ending and I know it is not

The Porch

Two evergreens taller than the house
have grown beyond this porch,
taller than the second floor.
Here, I am not afraid. It is true.
Only at night can the twister inside return.
Here, the porch is solid, well-built.
Everything solid, until I think of Ally,
who after Paul's preventable death,
volunteered to feed soldiers thousands of miles away.
She returned from her stint as someone else
determined to die and she did.
Here, mushrooms the size of dessert plates
grow in pairs. Where do I belong?
From the beginning, the air told me:
The white wicker bench with silk pillows is enough.
Stink bugs and frogs below enough.
Don't listen for footsteps that ask you to care.
Meanwhile, hummingbirds battle for sugared water.
They disappear and return, I suppose, to their secreted nest.
I made the mistake of reading a headline: Novelist reports rape.
She will be listened to, unlike a maid from Guinea.
I imagine that here, by the mountain,
hurt is expected and understood.
I listen to the hummingbird's warning.
The river below is impossible to find without directions.
My body curls into the wicker.
I don't know my country anymore

Notes on the Poems

Trying To Speak To You

> *Death Seizes a Woman* (*Tod packt eine Frau*) from the series *Death* (*Tod*) Käthe Kollwitz (German, 1867–1945)

Reading the News

> *Xagaa*: Somalia dry season July – September
> *Naja haje*: Egyptian Cobra

Celebrate

> *We haven't seen each other for so long. I have so much to tell you.*
>   - Aung San Suu Kyi

> *won't you celebrate with me*
> *what i have shaped*
> *into a kind of life?*
>   - Lucille Clifton, "won't you celebrate with me"

About the Author

Amy Small-McKinney has published two chapbooks of poetry, *Body of Surrender* (2004) and *Clear Moon, Frost* (2009), both with Finishing Line Press. Her work has appeared in numerous journals, among them *The Cortland Review*, *The Pedestal Magazine*, *upstreet*, *Blue Fifth Review*, *SAND Berlin's English Literary Journal*, *Switchback* (U of SF), and *LIPS Magazine*. In Fall 2012, her poem "Nighttime, Enigma, and Nostalgia," was nominated by *Switchback* for the Sundress Publications' Best of the Net 2012.

A nominee for the Pushcart Prize in 2004 and again in 2006, she was the 2011 Montgomery County Poet Laureate, selected by Christopher Bursk. At the 2011 Massachusetts Poetry Festival, she was part of a collaboration of women artists and poets for the project, The Poetry Dress.

Founder of the program, Finding Our Voices: Poetry & Resilience, Amy Small-McKinney promotes the use of poetry to help others, particularly those struggling with mental health, to find their voices.

She lives in Blue Bell, PA with her husband, and is mother to a college student.

Colophon

The body of *Life is Perfect* is set in several styles and weights of Adobe Minion, created by master calligrapher and type designer Robert Slimbach. Released in several versions between 1990 and 2000, Minion is inspired by classical, Old Style typefaces of the late Renaissance, a period of elegant, beautiful, and highly readable type designs. Crisp and open, it politely defers to the text, and allows itself to serve as a vehicle without adding its own statement.

Titles and headings are set in Agfa Rotis Semi Serif, a unique hybrid with characteristics of both serif and sans-serif faces. It is one member of a family of four fonts designed by Otl Aicher, and named after the village in the Allgäu where he has lived since 1972.

The BookArts Press logo is set in Linotype Zapfino, a tour-de-force of type design, a truly calligraphic face with a vast number of variants for most characters, including decorative ("swash") characters like the ampersand ('&') in our logo. Its creator, Hermann Zapf, is universally regarded as one of the greatest calligraphers and type designers of all time. Zapfino has the unique ability to function with equal facility in the most formal and the most informal settings.

Advance Critical Praise for

Life is Perfect

I have admired the poems of Amy Small-McKinney for years. She searches difficult regions and returns with wisdom and wonder. This she renders with concision, accuracy and brilliant language. She is one of the best poets we have.

    -Leonard Gontarek, Author of *Zen For Beginners*

In the title poem of *Life is Perfect*, Amy Small-McKinney, tells her daughter "we have to love what we are given – /the molecules or atoms that stabilize into ourselves." This is poetry that is atomic. Each poem quietly explodes on the page till you're watching a sparkler unfold its clusters of stars, so many linguistic excitements going on at once, you grieve each poem's end but can't wait for the next one to ignite. But the poetry here is atomic in another sense as well; it embraces life at its most essential, perfect in its imperfections: the tent kept in the living room, huge, questionable birds, Lemon Boy Hybrids, Bloodroot, unruly grass, the voices of the Rift Valley, of Merewala, of Bombay, Aunt Henrietta's *Art Nouveau – Jugendstil*, massive burritos, stuffed with "seasonings we haven't tasted before." In *Life is Perfect* we are offered spices we haven't tasted before, a feast we will never forget, poems whose adventures make us braver than we thought we could be – and wiser too!

    - Christopher Bursk, Author of *Improbable Swervings of Atoms*

In *Life is Perfect*, Amy Small-McKinney explores the inner and outer psychological landscape of family relations and our own connections to each other and ourselves. In luminous lyrical language, she proves she is a master of surrealistic leaps and startling metaphors. Her poems are haunting, often with a rare and rich thought-provoking layered quality but always emotionally truthful and with a purity of spirit that makes one want to return to these poems again and again. Small-McKinney is an exquisite poet and *Life is Perfect* is one of the most beautiful books of poetry I have read this year.

    - Laura Boss, Editor of *Lips*, Author of *Flashlight*

Also by Amy Small-McKinney

Clear Moon, Frost
Finishing Line Press (2009)

The poems in Amy Small-McKinney's chapbook, *Clear Moon, Frost*, take the world we think we know all too well, and return it to us, reordered, inside out, and bristling with wonder. Her sumptuous surreality taps directly into dream. Her wise metaphors are the gold that comes from walking into the furnace of life-and-death experiences with true faith. Humility and intensity are her hallmarks. Amy Small-McKinney writes with a commitment to inner life, inner depth, and inner truth.

– Molly Peacock

Amy Small-McKinney is a very wonderful poet, and has secretly and quietly produced some of the most beautiful poems I have ever read. Her poem, Letter From a Scarred & Aging Body, is so poignant it makes me seasick.

– Franz Wright

Body of Surrender
Finishing Line Press (2004)

There is a lush hush to these poems, as if the words of them were tapping on a wall between one's living room and the subconscious. Amy Small-McKinney's debut chapbook, *Body of Surrender*, introduces a wonderful poet of wisdom and tenderness, of murmured voices and measured silences.

– Kelly Cherry

It was said of Virgil that he brought forth his verses like a bear, and after formed them by licking. Amy Small-McKinney licks these poems from lumps of memory and desire into heart-scalding forms that have power and dignity and grace. She has taken the dust and breathed into it, inspired it. The poems are tough-minded and come from an informed heart.

– Bruce Smith

Body of Surrender explores inner and outer realms, the family and the world, the psyche's reach of memory and desire, in a voice which is both lyrical and blunt. The music of her language and the striking honesty of her insights are sources of real pleasure to a reader of these poems.

– Sandra Kohler

www.ingramcontent.com/pod-product-compliance
Lightning Source LLC
Chambersburg PA
CBHW081500040426
42446CB00016B/3328